Italian Alps Guide Book

Explore the Dolomites, Lake Como, and other Italian Alpine destinations.

Michael Bradley

Table of Contents

Chapter 1. Introduction to the Italian Alps

Overview of the Region

The Italian Alps stretch majestically across northern Italy, forming a natural border with neighboring countries such as France, Switzerland, Austria, and Slovenia. This region encompasses some of the most picturesque landscapes in Europe, with snow-capped peaks, verdant valleys, serene lakes, and charming alpine villages. Known for their dramatic beauty and cultural richness, the Italian Alps are a magnet for outdoor enthusiasts, history buffs, and travelers seeking tranquility or adventure. The Alps are divided into several distinct areas, including the Dolomites, the Aosta Valley, Lombardy, and Trentino-Alto Adige, each offering its unique charm and attractions.

Beyond their natural splendor, the Italian Alps are steeped in history, reflecting centuries of human settlement and cultural exchange. This region has seen the influence of ancient Roman legions, medieval traders, and even modern tourists. Today, the Italian Alps are celebrated not just for their visual appeal but also for their rich cultural tapestry, culinary heritage, and a wealth of outdoor activities, making them an ideal destination for travelers of all kinds.

Geographical Highlights

The Italian Alps boast an extraordinary range of geographical features, making them a playground for nature lovers and adventurers. One of the most iconic subranges is the Dolomites, recognized as a UNESCO World Heritage site for their jagged limestone peaks and breathtaking landscapes. These mountains are renowned for their striking alpenglow phenomenon, where the peaks turn shades of pink and orange during sunrise and sunset.

Another geographical highlight is the Monte Rosa massif, home to some of the highest peaks in the Alps. This area offers excellent mountaineering opportunities and features the famous Gorner Glacier, a must-see for adventurers and photographers. The Aosta Valley, nestled in the northwest, is another gem, surrounded by towering mountains such as Mont Blanc, the highest peak in Europe, and the Matterhorn, an iconic symbol of alpine grandeur.

Lake Garda, the largest lake in Italy, lies at the southern foothills of the Alps, blending alpine and Mediterranean climates. Its shores are dotted with picturesque towns, making it a perfect destination for a mix of relaxation and exploration. Additionally, the Stelvio Pass, one of Europe's highest mountain roads, offers hairpin turns and panoramic views that attract motor enthusiasts and cyclists from around the world.

Best Times to Visit

The Italian Alps are a year-round destination, with each season offering distinct experiences. Winter, from December to March, is ideal for snow sports enthusiasts. Renowned ski resorts like Cortina d'Ampezzo and Madonna di Campiglio offer world-class skiing, snowboarding, and après-ski activities. The snowy landscapes also set the stage for cozy stays in alpine lodges and festive Christmas markets.

Spring, from April to June, sees the region transform as snow melts to reveal lush green meadows and blooming wildflowers. This is a fantastic time for hiking, cycling, and exploring the quieter trails before the summer crowds arrive. Temperatures are mild, and the air is crisp, making outdoor activities particularly enjoyable.

Summer, from July to September, is perfect for those who love outdoor adventures. The mountains come alive with hikers, climbers, and cyclists eager to explore the alpine terrain. Lakes such as Como and Garda are popular for swimming, boating, and relaxing in a Mediterranean-like atmosphere. Festivals celebrating local traditions, music, and cuisine also take place during this season.

Autumn, from October to November, offers a quieter and more reflective experience. The landscape transforms into a palette of golds, oranges, and reds as the leaves change, creating stunning scenery. This is an excellent time for photography, wine tasting, and experiencing the region's slower pace without the bustle of peak tourist seasons.

No matter when you visit, the Italian Alps promise unforgettable experiences, blending natural beauty with cultural richness, making them a destination that calls travelers back time and again.

Chapter 2. History and Culture of the Italian Alps

Ancient Origins

The history of the Italian Alps is as dramatic and layered as the peaks themselves. Archaeological evidence suggests human activity in the region dating back to the Paleolithic era, with early inhabitants surviving through hunting and foraging. By the Bronze Age, the Alps became a crossroads for trade, as evidenced by the discovery of tools, ornaments, and artifacts linking the region to distant cultures. One of the most fascinating discoveries is Ötzi the Iceman, a mummified man found in the Ötztal Alps, who lived around 3300 BCE. His well-preserved remains and belongings provide a unique glimpse into the life of early alpine inhabitants.

The ancient Celts also played a significant role in shaping the region. Their settlements introduced innovations in agriculture and metallurgy, which were crucial for survival in the harsh alpine environment. By the time the Roman Empire expanded into the Alps around the 2nd century BCE, the region became a vital passage for trade and military campaigns. The Romans constructed roads, fortified towns, and left a legacy of engineering marvels, some of which, like the ancient road networks, remain visible today.

Influence of Neighboring Cultures

The Italian Alps have long served as a cultural melting pot, influenced by their proximity to France, Switzerland, Austria, and Slovenia. During the Middle Ages, the region witnessed the rise of independent alpine communities, often centered around monasteries and fortified villages. These communities thrived by adapting to the challenging environment, fostering unique architectural styles, and cultivating trade routes that connected northern and southern Europe.

The French influence is particularly evident in the Aosta Valley, where French is still widely spoken, and the region's architecture and culinary traditions reflect its close ties to Savoy. Germanic and Austrian cultural elements are predominant in Trentino-Alto Adige, where the German language is officially recognized, and traditional Tyrolean customs, such as yodeling and folk dances, are celebrated. Meanwhile, the Dolomites, with their Ladin-speaking population, represent a fascinating blend of Italian and ancient Rhaeto-Romanic cultures.

The Renaissance brought a wave of artistic and intellectual influence to the region, as alpine towns like Bolzano and Trento became important centers of learning and cultural exchange. This era also saw the construction of ornate churches, castles, and public buildings, many of which still stand as a testament to the region's historical significance.

Modern Traditions and Alpine Lifestyle

In the modern era, the Italian Alps continue to embody a rich cultural identity, rooted in tradition yet embracing contemporary influences. Alpine festivals, often tied to the changing seasons, remain an integral part of life. For instance, springtime festivals celebrate the return of livestock to mountain pastures, while autumn harvest festivals honor the bounty of the land. These events are opportunities for communities to come together and preserve their heritage through music, dance, and storytelling.

The culinary traditions of the Italian Alps are another cornerstone of the region's culture. Locally produced cheeses, such as Fontina from the Aosta Valley and Asiago from Veneto, are staples of alpine cuisine. Polenta, hearty stews, and cured meats also feature prominently, reflecting the resourcefulness of communities in utilizing seasonal and locally sourced ingredients.

Daily life in the Alps is often centered around nature, with a strong emphasis on sustainability and living in harmony with the environment. Many villages rely on eco-tourism and traditional crafts, such as woodcarving, weaving, and pottery, to support their economies. The architectural style of alpine homes, characterized by steeply pitched roofs and wooden facades, is both practical and a nod to centuries-old building techniques.

In recent decades, the Italian Alps have also become a hub for modern sports and leisure activities, from world-class skiing to cycling. Yet, despite the influx of global visitors, the region has managed to preserve its unique identity. Whether through the sound of cowbells echoing in the valleys, the sight of traditional dirndls and lederhosen during festivals, or the taste of a lovingly prepared alpine meal, the culture of the Italian Alps remains a rich and integral part of its allure.

The history and culture of the Italian Alps offer a captivating journey through time, revealing a region that has adapted to change while fiercely guarding its traditions. It is this delicate balance that makes the Italian Alps not just a place of extraordinary natural beauty but also a living, breathing testament to human resilience and creativity.

Chapter 3.Top Destinations in the Italian Alps

Dolomites

The Dolomites, a UNESCO World Heritage Site, are among the most iconic and striking mountain ranges in the world. Located in northeastern Italy, they span the provinces of South Tyrol, Trentino, and Belluno, offering a unique blend of breathtaking landscapes, outdoor activities, and cultural richness. Known for their jagged limestone peaks, the Dolomites are especially famous for the "enrosadira," a natural phenomenon that bathes the mountains in hues of pink, orange, and purple at sunrise and sunset.

One of the highlights of the Dolomites is the Tre Cime di Lavaredo, a trio of towering peaks that are a must-see for hikers and climbers. The area offers a variety of trails, ranging from easy walks suitable for families to challenging ascents for experienced adventurers. During winter, the Dolomites transform into a snow sports paradise, with ski resorts like Cortina d'Ampezzo and Val Gardena offering world-class slopes and facilities.

Beyond outdoor pursuits, the Dolomites are home to charming villages such as Ortisei and Canazei, where visitors can experience Ladin culture, a unique blend of Italian, Austrian, and ancient Rhaeto-Romanic traditions. The local cuisine is equally diverse, with dishes like canederli (bread dumplings), speck (smoked ham), and strudel showcasing the region's culinary heritage.

Whether you're seeking adrenaline-pumping adventures or tranquil moments in nature, the Dolomites are a destination that leaves an indelible impression.

Aosta Valley

Nestled in northwestern Italy, the Aosta Valley is a picturesque region surrounded by some of the highest peaks in the Alps, including Mont Blanc, Monte Rosa, and the Matterhorn. This region is a haven for outdoor enthusiasts, history lovers, and anyone seeking a blend of natural beauty and cultural depth.

The Aosta Valley is renowned for its castles, with over 100 dotting the landscape. The imposing Fenis Castle and the medieval Sarre Castle are among the most visited, offering insights into the region's storied past. The Roman influence is also evident in the town of Aosta, often referred to as the "Rome of the Alps," where visitors can explore well-preserved ruins such as the Arch of Augustus and the Roman Theatre.

For outdoor activities, the Aosta Valley is unmatched. Skiing and snowboarding are popular during winter, with resorts like Courmayeur and Cervinia attracting visitors from across the globe. In summer, the valley offers excellent hiking and trekking routes, including trails that lead to breathtaking glaciers and alpine lakes. The Gran Paradiso National Park, Italy's oldest national park, is a must-visit for wildlife enthusiasts, home to ibex, marmots, and golden eagles.

The region's culinary scene is equally appealing, with specialties such as Fontina cheese, polenta, and game meats reflecting its alpine roots. Aosta Valley's wines, particularly its robust reds, are the perfect accompaniment to any meal. This combination of history, natural beauty, and gastronomy makes the Aosta Valley a standout destination in the Italian Alps.

Trentino-Alto Adige

Trentino-Alto Adige, located in the northernmost part of Italy, is a region of contrasts, where Italian and Austrian influences merge to create a distinctive cultural and natural experience. The region is divided into two provinces: Trentino to the south, with its Italian character, and Alto Adige (or South Tyrol) to the north, where Germanic traditions are predominant.

Trento, the capital of Trentino, is a vibrant city known for its Renaissance architecture and historical significance as the site of the Council of Trent. Visitors can explore landmarks such as the Buonconsiglio Castle and the Trento Cathedral while enjoying the city's lively atmosphere. In South Tyrol, the city of Bolzano serves as the gateway to the Dolomites and is famous for its archaeological museum, which houses the mummified remains of Ötzi the Iceman.

The region's natural beauty is unparalleled, with crystal-clear lakes like Lake Caldaro and Lake Resia, lush vineyards, and sprawling apple orchards. During winter, resorts like Val di Fassa and Alta Badia offer excellent skiing opportunities, while summer visitors can enjoy hiking, cycling, and exploring the region's alpine pastures.

Trentino-Alto Adige is also a culinary delight, blending Italian and Austrian flavors. Traditional dishes include Schlutzkrapfen (spinach and ricotta-filled pasta), knödel (dumplings), and hearty stews, often paired with local wines or craft beers. The region's Christmas markets, particularly in Bolzano and Merano, add a magical touch during the holiday season, attracting visitors with their festive ambiance and artisanal goods.

From its diverse landscapes and rich history to its unique cultural fusion, Trentino-Alto Adige offers something for every traveler, making it an essential stop on any journey through the Italian Alps.

Chapter 4. Outdoor Activities and Adventures

Skiing and Snowboarding Hotspots

The Italian Alps are synonymous with skiing and snowboarding, boasting some of the best slopes in Europe. From world-class resorts to hidden gems, the region caters to beginners and seasoned enthusiasts alike. Cortina d'Ampezzo, often called the "Queen of the Dolomites," is one of Italy's most renowned ski destinations. Host of the 2026 Winter Olympics, it offers a vast network of pistes surrounded by breathtaking scenery. The resort's après-ski scene is equally appealing, with stylish bars and restaurants perfect for unwinding after a day on the slopes.

For families and intermediate skiers, the Val di Fassa in Trentino is an excellent choice. Its well-groomed trails, modern lifts, and welcoming atmosphere make it a favorite among those looking for a balanced ski experience. Meanwhile, advanced skiers can test their skills at the Stelvio Pass Glacier, one of the few places in Europe where skiing is possible year-round.

Cervinia, located in the Aosta Valley, offers a unique experience with its high-altitude slopes and connection to Zermatt in Switzerland. This resort is famous for its long runs and reliable snow cover. Those seeking a more budget-friendly yet high-quality option can head to Bormio in Lombardy, known for its thermal spas, making it an ideal destination for combining adventure and relaxation.

Hiking and Trekking Trails

When the snow melts, the Italian Alps reveal a vast network of hiking and trekking trails, offering adventures for all levels of fitness and experience. The Alta Via routes in the Dolomites are particularly popular, with well-marked trails that traverse dramatic landscapes of towering peaks, verdant meadows, and serene alpine lakes. Alta Via 1, known as the "Classic Trek," is a favorite among hikers for its manageable difficulty and stunning views.

For those seeking a more challenging adventure, the Gran Paradiso National Park in the Aosta Valley offers high-altitude trails that reward trekkers with views of glaciers and encounters with wildlife such as ibex and chamois. The Tour du Mont Blanc, a legendary long-distance trek, passes through the Italian side of Mont Blanc, offering unparalleled panoramas and the opportunity to explore charming alpine villages along the way.

Families and casual hikers will enjoy trails like the Puez-Odle Nature Park loop in South Tyrol, which offers moderate paths with breathtaking vistas of the Dolomites. Lake Como and Lake Garda also provide picturesque routes along their shores, combining hiking with the opportunity to relax by the water. Each trail in the Italian Alps offers a unique experience, from challenging summits to gentle walks through wildflower-strewn meadows.

Rock Climbing and Via Ferrata

The Italian Alps are a climber's paradise, with rock formations ranging from beginner-friendly crags to technical climbs that challenge even the most experienced. The Dolomites, in particular, are world-famous for their climbing routes, offering limestone walls and spires that attract climbers from across the globe. Areas such as Cinque Torri and Marmolada are must-visit spots for traditional and sport climbing enthusiasts.

For those seeking an adrenaline rush without the complexities of traditional climbing, the Italian Alps are home to an extensive network of via ferrata routes. These "iron paths" are equipped with fixed cables, ladders, and bridges, allowing climbers to navigate vertical rock faces and exposed ridges safely. Via ferrata routes originated in the Dolomites during World War I as a means for soldiers to traverse difficult terrain, and they now provide a thrilling way to explore the mountains.

One of the most famous via ferrata routes is the Via Ferrata delle Bocchette in the Brenta Dolomites. This multi-day adventure takes climbers through dramatic rock formations and offers jaw-dropping views at every turn. For families and beginners, simpler routes like those near Lake Garda offer a gentler introduction to via ferrata while still providing an exciting experience.

The Italian Alps also offer opportunities for bouldering, ice climbing, and canyoning, ensuring that adventure seekers have no shortage of options. Guided tours and climbing schools are readily available, making it easy for visitors to participate regardless of their skill level.

Whether skiing down pristine slopes, trekking through verdant valleys, or scaling rugged peaks, the outdoor activities and adventures in the Italian Alps provide an exhilarating way to connect with nature and experience the region's unparalleled beauty.

Chapter 5.Winter Wonderland: Snow Sports in the Italian Alps

Top Ski Resorts

The Italian Alps are a haven for snow sports

enthusiasts, offering an array of world-class ski resorts with breathtaking scenery and top-notch facilities. Cortina d'Ampezzo in the Dolomites is one of the most renowned resorts, often referred to as the "Queen of the Dolomites." Known for its glamorous atmosphere and stunning pistes, Cortina also offers a lively après-ski scene, high-end shopping, and excellent dining options. It's a favorite destination for both casual skiers and professionals, having hosted numerous international skiing events.

Another standout is Madonna di Campiglio in Trentino, a charming resort with a vast network of ski runs catering to all skill levels. Its connection to the Dolomiti di Brenta circuit allows skiers to explore a variety of terrains amidst spectacular alpine vistas. The resort is also famous for its snowboarding parks, making it a hotspot for freestyle enthusiasts.

For those seeking high-altitude thrills, Cervinia in the Aosta Valley is unparalleled. Linked with Zermatt in Switzerland, it provides access to some of the longest ski runs in Europe, including slopes on the iconic Matterhorn. Bormio, located in Lombardy, combines exceptional skiing with rejuvenating thermal baths, making it an ideal destination for those who want to unwind after an active day on the slopes.

Families and beginners will appreciate resorts like Livigno, known for its friendly atmosphere, gentle slopes, and tax-free shopping. Each resort in the Italian Alps offers something unique, ensuring that every visitor can find the perfect winter escape.

Tips for Beginners and Experts

For beginners, choosing the right resort and preparing adequately can make all the difference. Resorts like Livigno and San Martino di Castrozza are excellent starting points, with wide, gentle slopes and accessible ski schools offering lessons from certified instructors. Renting equipment instead of purchasing is a practical option for first-timers, and booking lessons in advance can save time and ensure availability. Wearing proper gear, including layered clothing, waterproof gloves, and a helmet, is crucial for comfort and safety.

Intermediate and expert skiers should explore resorts offering diverse terrains and challenging runs. Cervinia's high-altitude pistes and Madonna di Campiglio's technical slopes are ideal for advanced skiers seeking a thrill. Those venturing into off-piste areas should prioritize safety, carrying avalanche gear, and hiring a local guide familiar with the terrain.

Regardless of skill level, it's essential to respect mountain etiquette, such as staying in control on crowded slopes, yielding to downhill skiers, and avoiding abrupt stops in narrow passages. Adapting to changing weather conditions and keeping hydrated are equally important for an enjoyable day on the slopes.

Off-Piste Adventures

For thrill-seekers, the Italian Alps offer an abundance of off-piste opportunities, from untouched powder fields to challenging descents in remote areas. The Monte Rosa massif, shared between the Aosta Valley and Piedmont, is a premier destination for backcountry skiing. It boasts vast terrain with deep powder and breathtaking views, accessible through guided tours and helicopter skiing.

The Sella Ronda, a renowned ski circuit in the Dolomites, also offers off-piste adventures for those looking to explore beyond the marked trails. Expert guides can lead skiers to lesser-known routes through pristine alpine wilderness, providing an exhilarating experience for advanced enthusiasts.

Freeriders will find paradise in Livigno, with its abundant powder and specially designated off-piste zones. Snowboarders can enjoy open bowls and challenging tree runs, while skiers tackle steep descents that test their skills and endurance.

For a truly unique experience, consider night skiing, available at select resorts like Cortina d'Ampezzo and Madonna di Campiglio. Gliding under the stars on illuminated slopes is an unforgettable way to enjoy the Italian Alps' winter magic. Alternatively, try snowshoeing or ski touring, which offer quieter ways to explore off-piste areas and connect with the pristine beauty of the mountains.

Safety is paramount for off-piste adventures. Avalanches are a real risk, so skiers and snowboarders must carry essential safety equipment, including a transceiver, probe, and shovel. Joining a guided tour is strongly recommended, as experienced guides can navigate challenging conditions and ensure a safe and enjoyable outing.

The Italian Alps provide endless opportunities for snow sports, from thrilling descents and freestyle tricks to serene tours through unspoiled landscapes. Whether you're a novice eager to learn or an expert seeking adrenaline-pumping challenges, this winter wonderland promises unforgettable experiences.

Chapter 6. Summertime Escapes in the Alps

Lakes and Alpine Meadows

When the snow melts, the Italian Alps transform into a vibrant summer paradise, where emerald lakes and lush alpine meadows beckon visitors seeking tranquility and natural beauty. Iconic lakes like Lake Garda, Lake Como, and Lake Maggiore are just a stone's throw from the alpine peaks, offering the perfect blend of dramatic mountain views and serene waters. Lake Garda, the largest lake in Italy, is particularly popular for its crystal-clear waters and charming lakeside towns like Malcesine and Riva del Garda. Here, visitors can swim, sail, or simply relax on the shores while soaking in the Mediterranean-like ambiance.

High in the mountains, smaller alpine lakes like Lago di Braies and Lago di Sorapis offer breathtaking scenery. Lago di Braies, often dubbed the "Pearl of the Dolomites," captivates visitors with its turquoise waters framed by rugged peaks, making it a favorite spot for photography and gentle hiking. Meanwhile, the meadows of the Seiser Alm, Europe's largest high-altitude plateau, come alive with wildflowers during the summer months, offering endless opportunities for picnics, leisurely walks, and horseback riding.

For those looking to connect with nature, many mountain huts (or rifugi) in the Alps provide rustic accommodations surrounded by unspoiled landscapes. Staying in these huts is an authentic way to experience the region, with hearty local meals and unparalleled stargazing opportunities.

Cycling and Mountain Biking Routes

The Italian Alps are a dream destination for cyclists, offering everything from challenging mountain passes to scenic trails for leisurely rides. The Stelvio Pass, one of the most famous cycling routes in the world, is a must for serious cyclists. This legendary climb, with its 48 hairpin bends, rewards riders with panoramic views and a profound sense of accomplishment. Another iconic route is the Gavia Pass, known for its grueling ascent and dramatic alpine scenery. Both routes are staples of the Giro d'Italia, attracting cycling enthusiasts from across the globe.

For mountain bikers, the Dolomites offer a wealth of trails catering to all skill levels. The Sella Ronda MTB tour is particularly popular, providing a thrilling circuit around the Sella massif with the option of using cable cars to assist with ascents. South Tyrol also boasts an extensive network of trails, from gentle vineyard paths to adrenaline-pumping downhill tracks. Livigno, often called the "Little Tibet" of Italy, is a hotspot for mountain biking, with dedicated bike parks and over 3,200 kilometers of mapped trails.

Families and casual cyclists will enjoy the Adige River cycling path, which winds through picturesque valleys and historic towns like Bolzano and Trento. Renting an e-bike is a great way to explore the region's hilly terrain without breaking a sweat, making the Alps accessible to riders of all abilities.

Paragliding and Adventure Sports

For adrenaline junkies, the Italian Alps offer an array of adventure sports, with paragliding being one of the most popular summer activities. Flying high above the valleys, paragliders are treated to awe-inspiring views of the rugged peaks, verdant forests, and glistening lakes below. Monte Baldo, near Lake Garda, is one of the top spots for paragliding, offering tandem flights for beginners and experienced pilots alike. The experience of soaring like a bird, accompanied by the silent majesty of the mountains, is truly unforgettable.

Other adventure sports abound, including canyoning, which involves navigating waterfalls and gorges through a combination of climbing, swimming, and rappelling. In the Dolomites, Val di Sole and the Sarca Valley are prime locations for this thrilling activity.

For those seeking a challenge, rock climbing and via ferrata routes are abundant in the summer months. The Dolomites are especially renowned for their via ferrata paths, which provide an exhilarating way to scale the mountains using fixed cables and ladders. The Brenta

Dolomites' Bocchette Route is a standout, offering a mix of adventure and breathtaking views.

Ziplining, whitewater rafting, and kayaking are also popular activities during the summer. In Val di Sole, the Noce River is ranked among the top rafting destinations in Europe, with rapids ranging from gentle to extreme. Meanwhile, the alpine streams and lakes provide serene spots for kayaking and stand-up paddleboarding.

Summertime in the Italian Alps is a season of boundless opportunity, offering everything from serene lakeside retreats to adrenaline-fueled adventures. Whether you're a nature lover, a sports enthusiast, or simply looking to escape the summer heat, the Italian Alps deliver an unforgettable experience under the sun.

Chapter 7. Charming Alpine Towns and Villages

The Italian Alps are not just about breathtaking peaks and thrilling outdoor adventures. They are also home to some of the most charming towns and villages in Europe, each offering a unique blend of history, culture, and natural beauty. This chapter will take you through Cortina d'Ampezzo, Bolzano and Merano, and Sestriere and its surroundings, giving you an in-depth look at what makes these destinations so captivating.

Cortina d'Ampezzo: The Queen of the Dolomites

Nestled in the heart of the Dolomites, Cortina d'Ampezzo is renowned for its stunning alpine landscapes and cosmopolitan atmosphere. This picturesque town is a magnet for outdoor enthusiasts, luxury seekers, and those looking to experience the magic of the Italian Alps.

Activities and Attractions:
Cortina offers world-class skiing and snowboarding in the winter, with slopes that cater to all skill levels. In the summer, the town transforms into a haven for hikers and climbers, with trails leading to iconic peaks such as Tofane and Cristallo. Don't miss the *Falzarego Pass*, which offers panoramic views and access to historical World War I sites.

Culture and Cuisine:
Beyond its natural beauty, Cortina boasts a vibrant cultural scene. Visit the *Regole Museum*, showcasing local art and history, or explore the charming streets lined with boutique shops selling traditional crafts and high-end fashion. For food lovers, Cortina's restaurants serve up a delightful mix of Italian and Tyrolean flavors. Try local specialties like *casunziei* (stuffed pasta) and polenta dishes paired with a robust red wine.

Where to Stay:
Cortina offers accommodations ranging from luxurious chalets to cozy bed-and-breakfasts. Top picks include the *Cristallo Resort & Spa* for an indulgent stay or *Hotel de la Poste* for a touch of alpine tradition.

Bolzano and Merano: A Cultural and Thermal Paradise

Bolzano and Merano, located in the South Tyrol region, combine the best of Italian and Austrian influences. These towns are a must-visit for their rich history, stunning landscapes, and therapeutic thermal baths.

Bolzano: Gateway to the Dolomites
Bolzano is famed for its vibrant blend of cultures, reflected in its architecture, language, and cuisine. The city is home to the *South Tyrol Museum of Archaeology*, where you can meet Ötzi the Iceman, a remarkably preserved mummy dating back over 5,000 years. Stroll through the *Piazza Walther* and admire the Gothic Bolzano Cathedral, or enjoy a glass of the region's famous Lagrein wine at a local enoteca.

Merano: The Spa Town
Merano is synonymous with relaxation, thanks to its renowned thermal baths. The *Terme Merano* offers modern spa facilities with a stunning alpine backdrop, making it a perfect retreat after a day of exploring. The town's mild climate and Mediterranean-style gardens provide a stark yet beautiful contrast to the towering peaks surrounding it.

Events and Festivals:
Both towns host lively events throughout the year, such as the *Bolzano Christmas Market*, where the streets come alive with lights, music, and the aroma of mulled wine, and the *Merano WineFestival*, a prestigious event celebrating local wines and gastronomy.

Where to Stay:
In Bolzano, consider *Parkhotel Laurin*, a historic hotel
with an elegant ambiance. In Merano, *Hotel Terme
Merano* offers direct access to the thermal baths, while
Castel Fragsburg provides a luxurious escape in a
castle setting.

Sestriere and Beyond: Alpine Adventures and Hidden Gems

Sestriere, located in the Piedmont region, is a prime
destination for sports enthusiasts and nature lovers
alike. As part of the *Via Lattea* (Milky Way) ski area, it
offers access to over 400 kilometers of interconnected
slopes.

Activities in Sestriere:
Sestriere is a hub for winter sports, hosting skiing and
snowboarding events of international renown, including
past Winter Olympic Games. In the summer, it becomes
a paradise for mountain bikers and golfers, with
Europe's highest 18-hole golf course.

Exploring Beyond Sestriere:
Venture into nearby villages like Sauze d'Oulx, Cesana
Torinese, and Pragelato, each offering unique alpine
experiences. Sauze d'Oulx is known for its vibrant
après-ski scene, while Pragelato charms visitors with its
traditional wooden chalets and serene nature reserves.

Local Delights:
The Piedmont region is celebrated for its culinary
offerings. Indulge in hearty mountain dishes such as
bagna càuda (a warm anchovy and garlic dip) and local

cheeses like *toma piemontese*. Pair your meal with a glass of Barolo or Barbera wine.

Where to Stay:
In Sestriere, options range from luxury resorts like the *Principi di Piemonte* to family-friendly lodges. For a more secluded experience, consider staying in a rustic chalet in one of the neighboring villages.

The Italian Alps are not just a destination—they're an experience that blends natural beauty, culture, and adventure. Whether you're drawn to the glamour of Cortina, the cultural richness of Bolzano and Merano, or the adrenaline-filled slopes of Sestriere, these towns and villages promise memories that will last a lifetime.

Chapter 8. Natural Wonders and National Parks

The Italian Alps are a treasure trove of natural wonders, where breathtaking landscapes meet a commitment to preserving biodiversity. In this chapter, we'll explore the pristine beauty of Stelvio National Park, the majestic Adamello Brenta Nature Park, and the rich tapestry of wildlife and conservation efforts that make this region a haven for nature enthusiasts.

Stelvio National Park: Italy's Alpine Giant

Stelvio National Park, established in 1935, is one of Italy's largest and oldest national parks. Spanning the Lombardy and Trentino-Alto Adige regions, the park offers visitors a stunning mix of rugged mountains, verdant valleys, and glacial wonders.

Scenic Highlights:
The park is dominated by the Ortler-Cevedale massif, home to some of the highest peaks in the Eastern Alps. The *Stelvio Pass*, one of Europe's most famous mountain roads, winds through the park, offering jaw-dropping views and thrilling hairpin turns. Don't miss the glaciers of the Forni Valley, a surreal landscape of ice and rock.

Outdoor Activities:
Stelvio National Park is a paradise for adventure seekers. Hiking trails range from gentle paths like the *Val Martello Nature Trail* to challenging ascents for

seasoned climbers. In winter, the park transforms into a haven for skiers and snowshoers. Cyclists flock to Stelvio Pass for the ultimate test of endurance on its steep and winding route.

Flora and Fauna:
The park's diverse ecosystems are home to unique alpine flora such as edelweiss and gentian. Wildlife enthusiasts can spot ibex, chamois, and red deer, as well as golden eagles soaring above the peaks. The park also plays a critical role in the conservation of rare species like the bearded vulture.

Adamello Brenta Nature Park: A UNESCO Treasure

Located in Trentino, the Adamello Brenta Nature Park is a UNESCO Global Geopark celebrated for its geological diversity, sparkling lakes, and lush forests.

The Brenta Dolomites:
The park's crown jewel is the Brenta Dolomites, a dramatic range of towering limestone peaks that glow pink at sunset. This area is a climber's dream, with via ferrata routes providing access to spectacular vistas.

Lake Expeditions:
The park is dotted with over 80 picturesque lakes. *Lago di Tovel* is perhaps the most famous, known for its vibrant red algae blooms in the past, which earned it the nickname "Lake of Blood." Today, its turquoise waters and surrounding forests make it a perfect spot for a peaceful day trip.

Biodiversity:
Adamello Brenta is one of the few places in Italy where brown bears still roam freely. Efforts to reintroduce these majestic creatures have been a conservation success story. The park also boasts a rich array of bird species, including black woodpeckers and ptarmigans.

Eco-Friendly Adventures:
Visitors are encouraged to explore the park sustainably. Guided tours offer insights into the park's geology and wildlife, while eco-lodges and educational centers promote conservation awareness.

Wildlife and Conservation: Preserving the Alpine Ecosystem

The Italian Alps are home to a remarkable variety of wildlife, much of which is protected through conservation efforts in national parks and reserves.

Iconic Species:
The Alps are a sanctuary for species like the ibex, which was once on the brink of extinction but has made a remarkable recovery. Chamois and marmots are commonly spotted in alpine meadows, while lynxes and wolves are making a cautious return to the region.

Birdlife:
Birdwatchers will be delighted by the diversity of avian species. The golden eagle is a symbol of the Alps, often seen soaring above the peaks. Other notable birds include the alpine chough and the elusive rock ptarmigan.

Conservation Challenges:
Climate change poses significant threats to the Alps, with shrinking glaciers and changing ecosystems affecting both wildlife and local communities. National parks like Stelvio and Adamello Brenta play a crucial role in mitigating these impacts through habitat protection, wildlife corridors, and educational initiatives.

How You Can Help:
Visitors can contribute to conservation by respecting park guidelines, staying on designated trails, and supporting local initiatives. Many parks offer volunteer programs, allowing nature lovers to actively participate in habitat restoration and wildlife monitoring.

The Italian Alps are a testament to the beauty and resilience of nature. Stelvio National Park and Adamello Brenta Nature Park, along with their incredible wildlife, stand as shining examples of the importance of preserving these precious landscapes for future generations. Whether you're hiking through glacial valleys, marveling at the Dolomites, or spotting a rare bird in the wild, these natural wonders promise unforgettable experiences.

Chapter 9. Gastronomy of the Italian Alps

The Italian Alps are a culinary haven where rich traditions meet the bounty of the mountains. The gastronomy here reflects the region's cultural diversity, blending Italian, Austrian, and Swiss influences into a unique and hearty cuisine. From traditional Alpine dishes to artisanal cheeses and world-class wines, dining in the Italian Alps is as memorable as its breathtaking landscapes.

Traditional Alpine Cuisine

The cuisine of the Italian Alps is shaped by its geography and history, emphasizing simple, robust flavors that warm both body and soul.

Hearty Dishes:
Traditional Alpine meals often center around staple ingredients like potatoes, grains, and cured meats, designed to sustain the high-altitude lifestyle.

Pizzoccheri, a type of buckwheat pasta mixed with potatoes, cabbage, and melted cheese, is a beloved dish in Lombardy. In Trentino, *canederli*—dumplings made with bread, speck, and herbs—are a must-try.

Polenta Variations:
Polenta, made from cornmeal, is a quintessential Alpine food. It can be served creamy alongside stews or baked and fried for a crispy treat. Pair it with *brasato al vino rosso* (wine-braised beef) or *capriolo in salmì* (venison stew) for a truly authentic experience.

Sweet Endings:
Alpine desserts are indulgent and satisfying. Look out for *strudel di mele*, a flaky apple strudel filled with raisins and cinnamon, or *zabaione al vino passito*, a rich egg-based dessert flavored with sweet wine.

Cheese, Wine, and Local Delicacies

The Italian Alps are home to some of the world's most prized cheeses and wines, alongside a variety of unique local products.

Artisanal Cheeses:
Cheese-making is a revered tradition in the Alps. *Fontina*, a creamy cheese from the Aosta Valley, is perfect for fondue, while *Taleggio* offers a mild, tangy flavor. Other regional specialties include *Bitto* from Valtellina and *Asiago* from the Veneto region. Visit a local dairy or *malga* (alpine hut) to sample these cheeses in their freshest form.

Wines of the Mountains:
The steep slopes of the Italian Alps are ideal for

cultivating vineyards that produce exceptional wines.
Trentino-Alto Adige is known for its crisp white wines
like *Gewürztraminer* and robust reds like *Lagrein*. In the
Aosta Valley, try *Fumin* or *Petit Rouge*, lesser-known
varietals with a distinct alpine character.

Cured Meats and Other Specialties:
The art of curing meats thrives in the Alps. *Speck*, a
smoked and spiced ham, is a regional favorite, often
enjoyed with crusty bread and cheese. Don't miss local
honey, chestnuts, and wild mushrooms, which add
seasonal flair to the cuisine.

Dining Experiences in the Mountains

The Italian Alps offer dining experiences that go beyond
the plate, combining stunning settings with exceptional
hospitality.

Mountain Huts and Rifugi:
Dining in a *rifugio* (mountain hut) is an unforgettable
experience. These rustic lodges, often perched high in
the mountains, serve traditional fare with a side of jaw-
dropping views. Popular dishes include polenta, hearty
soups, and locally sourced game. Rifugio Nuvolau in the
Dolomites is a favorite spot for its panoramic vistas and
authentic meals.

Farm-to-Table Restaurants:
The farm-to-table movement is alive and well in the
Alps, with many restaurants sourcing ingredients directly
from local farms. Restaurants like *Malga Panna* in
Trentino emphasize seasonal menus featuring the
freshest produce, meats, and cheeses.

Fine Dining and Michelin Stars:
For those seeking a more refined experience, the Italian Alps boast a selection of Michelin-starred restaurants. *St. Hubertus* in San Cassiano offers a creative take on mountain cuisine, while *La Siriola* blends innovation with tradition.

Après-Ski Delights:
No alpine dining experience is complete without après-ski indulgence. Warm up with a mug of *vin brulé* (mulled wine) or a shot of *grappa*, a potent spirit distilled from grape pomace. Pair your drink with *castagnaccio* (a chestnut cake) or freshly baked pastries.

Exploring Culinary Traditions

Food tours and cooking classes are an excellent way to immerse yourself in the gastronomy of the Italian Alps. Join a cheese-tasting tour in Valtellina, learn to make traditional dumplings in Bolzano, or explore wine cellars in Trentino.

The gastronomy of the Italian Alps is a celebration of the region's natural abundance and cultural heritage. Whether you're savoring a simple bowl of polenta in a mountain hut or enjoying a gourmet meal at a fine-dining restaurant, each bite tells a story of the land and its people. This culinary journey is one of the many reasons the Italian Alps remain an unforgettable destination.

Chapter 10. Festivals and Events in the Italian Alps

The Italian Alps are not only a haven for nature lovers but also a vibrant hub of cultural and festive activities. Throughout the year, the region hosts a diverse array of festivals and events that celebrate its unique traditions, seasonal splendor, and love for sports and adventure. This chapter highlights the most captivating celebrations that add a layer of excitement to any Alpine adventure.

Seasonal Celebrations

The changing seasons in the Italian Alps bring a variety of festivals that showcase the region's natural beauty, agricultural bounty, and festive spirit.

Spring Awakening:
In spring, Alpine meadows burst into bloom, and villages come alive with celebrations of renewal. The *Floribunda Festival* in the Dolomites is a must-visit for flower enthusiasts, featuring floral displays, guided hikes, and workshops on alpine flora.

Summer Festivals:
Summer is the season for outdoor festivities. The *Südtirol Jazz Festival Alto Adige* draws music lovers to open-air venues surrounded by mountains, while *Alpini Gatherings* celebrate the camaraderie of Italy's mountain troops with parades, music, and local fare.

Harvest and Autumn Events:
Autumn is a time to honor the land's bounty. The

Chestnut Festival in Valtellina showcases dishes made from freshly harvested chestnuts, alongside wine tastings and craft fairs. In Trentino, the *Grape Festival* features vineyard tours, grape stomping, and traditional dances.

Winter Wonderland:
Winter brings magical Christmas markets to Alpine towns like Bolzano and Merano. These markets feature artisan crafts, festive treats, and a warm holiday atmosphere. The *Krampus Night* in South Tyrol offers a unique twist, with costumed figures parading through the streets in a centuries-old tradition.

Unique Cultural Events

The Italian Alps are steeped in traditions that come to life through distinctive cultural festivals.

Carnival Celebrations:
Alpine villages host vibrant carnival festivities with a local twist. The *Carnival of Bagolino* in Lombardy features traditional masked dancers called *Balarì*, accompanied by live music. In Val di Fassa, the *Ladin Carnival* showcases ancient Ladin customs with colorful costumes and folklore performances.

Traditional Alpine Weddings:
Some villages, like Castelrotto, reenact traditional alpine weddings during festivals, complete with period costumes, horse-drawn carriages, and age-old rituals. Visitors are welcome to witness these ceremonies and join in the celebrations.

Folklore Festivals:
Folklore festivals are an opportunity to experience the region's heritage. The *Merano Folk Festival* offers a mix of traditional music, dance, and storytelling, while the *Settimana Ladina* in Val Gardena delves deep into Ladin culture with culinary events, art exhibits, and mountain excursions.

Sports and Adventure Festivals

The Italian Alps are a paradise for outdoor enthusiasts, and their festivals reflect a passion for adventure and athleticism.

Winter Sports Events:
Winter sports dominate the Alpine calendar. The *Sella Ronda Ski Marathon*, held in the Dolomites, is a thrilling night race that attracts top skiers from around the globe. Meanwhile, the *FIS Ski World Cup* regularly makes stops at renowned resorts like Cortina d'Ampezzo, showcasing elite skiing talent.

Summer Adventure Challenges:
In summer, the mountains become the setting for adventure races and outdoor challenges. The *Dolomiti Superbike* is a premier mountain biking event, offering demanding courses through spectacular terrain. Trail runners flock to the *Lavaredo Ultra Trail*, a grueling but rewarding race through the Dolomites.

Climbing and Mountaineering Celebrations:
Climbers and alpinists gather for festivals like the *Rock Master Festival* in Arco, which combines world-class climbing competitions with workshops and film screenings. The *International Mountain Film Festival* in

Trento celebrates the spirit of mountaineering through cinema.

Paragliding and Air Sports:
For those who love the skies, the *Paragliding Festival of Stelvio* offers breathtaking views and aerial competitions. Visitors can also take tandem flights to experience the Alps from above.

Planning Your Visit

To make the most of these festivals and events, plan your trip around the seasonal calendar. Many festivals have long-standing dates, such as the Christmas markets starting in late November or harvest festivals in September and October. Booking accommodations early is crucial, especially in smaller villages where availability is limited during major events.

Festivals and events in the Italian Alps offer a unique opportunity to connect with the region's traditions, culture, and adventurous spirit. Whether you're exploring a bustling Christmas market, dancing to traditional music, or cheering on athletes in a mountain race, these celebrations add unforgettable memories to your Alpine journey.

Chapter 11. Travel Tips for the Italian Alps

Traveling to the Italian Alps promises breathtaking landscapes, unforgettable experiences, and a wealth of activities to suit every traveler. To ensure a smooth and enjoyable journey, preparation is key. This chapter provides essential tips on packing, transportation, and safety for exploring this stunning mountainous region.

Packing Essentials

Packing for the Italian Alps depends on the season and the activities you plan to enjoy. However, there are a few universal items and considerations to keep in mind.

Seasonal Clothing:

- **Winter:** Insulated jackets, thermal layers, waterproof pants, gloves, hats, and sturdy snow boots are essential for skiing or winter hiking.

Don't forget sunglasses or goggles to protect against glare from the snow.
- **Summer:** Light layers for daytime hiking, a warm fleece or jacket for cooler evenings, and breathable, moisture-wicking clothing are ideal. A waterproof jacket is a must for sudden alpine rain showers.
- **Year-round:** Comfortable walking shoes or boots with good grip are indispensable.

Outdoor Gear:

- **Hiking:** Pack a daypack, a reusable water bottle, trekking poles, a first-aid kit, and a map or GPS device.
- **Winter Sports:** If you're skiing or snowboarding, you may choose to bring your own equipment or rent locally. Helmets, gloves, and a good base layer are non-negotiable.

Other Essentials:

- Sunscreen and lip balm with high SPF, as the sun's rays are stronger at higher altitudes.
- Adapters and chargers for electronics, as Italy uses the Type F or L plug.
- Snacks for day trips, such as nuts or energy bars, especially if you're venturing into remote areas.

Transportation and Getting Around

Navigating the Italian Alps can be as exciting as the destination itself. Understanding transportation options helps you plan effectively.

By Air:
Major airports like Milan Malpensa, Venice Marco Polo, and Verona Villafranca serve as gateways to the Alps. Regional airports such as Bolzano may also be convenient for certain destinations.

By Train:
Italy's rail network connects many towns and cities near the Alps, making train travel a scenic and efficient choice. Regional trains link cities like Trento, Bolzano, and Aosta with nearby mountain villages. Consider purchasing an *Eurail Pass* if you plan extensive train travel.

By Car:
Driving is one of the best ways to explore the Alps, offering flexibility and access to remote areas. Ensure your vehicle is equipped for mountain roads, especially in winter when snow chains may be required. Parking is readily available in most towns and ski resorts, though fees may apply.

Public Transportation:
Local buses operate in most Alpine regions, connecting towns, ski resorts, and trailheads. In some areas, cable cars and funiculars provide access to higher altitudes, such as in the Dolomites or the Aosta Valley.

Eco-Friendly Options:
Many Alpine regions promote sustainable travel. Look for electric shuttle services, bike rentals, and well-marked hiking trails that minimize environmental impact.

Safety Tips for Alpine Travel

Safety should always be a priority when exploring the Italian Alps, whether you're strolling through charming villages or embarking on high-altitude adventures.

Altitude Awareness:
If traveling to higher elevations, take time to acclimate to avoid altitude sickness. Stay hydrated, avoid alcohol, and ascend gradually if possible.

Weather Conditions:
The weather in the Alps can change rapidly. Check forecasts frequently and be prepared for sudden rain, snow, or temperature drops. In winter, watch for avalanche warnings if venturing off-piste.

Trail Safety:
Stick to marked trails and carry a map or GPS device. Inform someone of your plans if hiking alone and always have an emergency contact number handy.

Winter Sports Precautions:
Wear a helmet while skiing or snowboarding and follow posted signs and regulations. If you're new to a sport, consider taking lessons from a certified instructor.

Wildlife and Environment:
While wildlife encounters are rare, it's essential to respect local fauna. Do not feed or approach animals, and practice *Leave No Trace* principles to preserve the natural environment.

Health and Emergency Services:
Carry basic first-aid supplies and know the emergency

contact numbers for the region. Italy's emergency number is **112**, which connects to police, ambulance, and fire services. Consider purchasing travel insurance that includes coverage for outdoor activities and medical evacuation.

Final Tips for a Memorable Journey

- **Plan Ahead:** Popular destinations in the Italian Alps can book up quickly, especially during peak seasons. Reserve accommodations, tours, and transportation in advance.
- **Language and Etiquette:** While Italian is widely spoken, German and Ladin may also be common in some areas. Learning a few basic phrases can enhance your interactions with locals.
- **Stay Flexible:** The Alps are about embracing the moment. Whether you discover an unexpected festival or decide to linger at a scenic spot, leave room in your itinerary for spontaneity.

With the right preparation and a sense of adventure, the Italian Alps promise a safe and unforgettable travel experience. By packing wisely, navigating with ease, and staying vigilant about safety, you'll be ready to make the most of this extraordinary destination.

Chapter 12. Where to Stay in the Italian Alps

The Italian Alps offer a wide range of accommodations, catering to every type of traveler, from those seeking opulent luxury to adventurers on a budget. Choosing the right place to stay depends on your preferences, itinerary, and the level of comfort you desire. In this chapter, explore the best options for lodging in this stunning region, whether you're planning a romantic getaway, a family vacation, or a solo adventure.

Luxury Resorts and Hotels

For those who crave indulgence and top-tier amenities, the Italian Alps boast some of the most luxurious accommodations in Europe.

Five-Star Retreats:
Many of the region's luxury resorts offer breathtaking views, world-class service, and unique experiences. In Cortina d'Ampezzo, **Cristallo, a Luxury Collection Resort & Spa** combines modern elegance with historic charm, featuring an award-winning spa and gourmet dining. Similarly, **Lefay Resort & SPA Dolomiti** in Pinzolo is a haven for wellness enthusiasts, offering extensive spa facilities and eco-friendly design.

Ski-In/Ski-Out Hotels:
For avid skiers, staying in a ski-in/ski-out resort ensures convenience and maximizes time on the slopes. **Rosa Alpina Hotel & Spa** in San Cassiano provides direct access to the Dolomiti Superski area and offers luxurious rooms with Alpine décor. Another excellent option is **Hotel La Perla** in Corvara, known for its Michelin-starred restaurant and exceptional hospitality.

Historical and Boutique Stays:
Boutique hotels like **Hotel Chalet del Sogno** in Madonna di Campiglio combine intimate settings with a touch of luxury. Many of these establishments incorporate traditional architecture and personalized services, ensuring a memorable stay.

Cozy Alpine Chalets

For an authentic Alpine experience, staying in a chalet offers charm, privacy, and the chance to immerse yourself in the mountain lifestyle.

Traditional Chalets:
Alpine chalets, often built with local wood and stone, exude a rustic yet cozy ambiance. Many are located in picturesque villages or tucked away in serene valleys. **Chalet Eden** in La Thuile combines traditional design with modern comforts and eco-friendly practices.

Self-Catering Options:
Chalets with fully equipped kitchens are perfect for families or groups looking for flexibility. In Val di Fiemme, **Residence Aparthotel Des Alpes** offers spacious chalets with access to wellness facilities and recreational activities.

Luxury Chalets:
For a high-end experience, consider luxury chalets that come with private chefs, hot tubs, and dedicated staff. **San Lorenzo Mountain Lodge** near Brunico is a standout, offering exclusivity and unparalleled service in a beautifully restored hunting lodge.

Budget-Friendly Accommodations

Travelers on a budget will find plenty of options in the Italian Alps without compromising comfort or convenience.

Hostels and Guesthouses:
Hostels like **Ostello di Arco** in Trentino provide clean,

affordable lodging and a friendly atmosphere, making them ideal for solo travelers or backpackers. Similarly, family-run guesthouses such as **Garni Ciasa Urban** in Alta Badia offer personalized service at reasonable rates.

B&Bs and Farm Stays:
Bed and breakfasts, often run by locals, offer a more intimate and affordable alternative to hotels. Many B&Bs, such as **Casa Ai Conti** in the Aosta Valley, include homemade breakfasts featuring local products. Farm stays, like those offered through the **Agriturismo Sudtirolese** network, allow guests to experience rural life while enjoying hearty meals and scenic surroundings.

Budget Hotels:
Chains like **B&B Hotels** or smaller independent establishments in towns such as Bolzano and Trento cater to travelers seeking comfort on a budget. These hotels are often centrally located and provide easy access to public transportation and nearby attractions.

Tips for Choosing the Right Accommodation

Location Matters:
Decide whether you want to stay close to ski resorts, hiking trails, or charming villages. For example, Cortina d'Ampezzo is ideal for winter sports, while Bolzano offers easy access to cultural landmarks and vineyards.

Consider Seasonal Demand:
Accommodations in the Italian Alps can fill up quickly during peak seasons like Christmas, New Year, and

summer holidays. Book well in advance if traveling during these times to secure the best options.

Look for Deals and Packages:
Many hotels and chalets offer special packages that include activities like skiing, hiking tours, or spa treatments. Checking for deals can save money and enhance your overall experience.

Eco-Friendly Stays:
For environmentally conscious travelers, several lodgings in the Alps prioritize sustainability. Look for establishments with certifications such as *ClimaHotel* or those that use renewable energy and local materials.

The Italian Alps provide a diverse range of accommodations that cater to every preference and budget. Whether you're seeking the opulence of a five-star resort, the charm of a traditional chalet, or the affordability of a cozy guesthouse, you'll find a welcoming place to call home during your Alpine adventure.

Chapter 13. Planning Your Itinerary

The Italian Alps are a treasure trove of natural beauty, outdoor adventures, and cultural experiences. To make the most of your visit, a well-thought-out itinerary is essential. Whether you're planning a weeklong adventure, a quick weekend escape, or a personalized journey, this chapter offers guidance to suit every type of traveler.

Suggested One-Week Adventure

For a comprehensive exploration of the Italian Alps, a week provides just enough time to experience a mix of activities, landscapes, and towns.

Day 1: Arrival and Bolzano Exploration

- Arrive in Bolzano, the gateway to the Dolomites.
- Visit the South Tyrol Museum of Archaeology to see Ötzi the Iceman.
- Stroll through Piazza Walther and enjoy local wines at a traditional enoteca.

Day 2: Hiking in the Dolomites

- Head to the Seiser Alm (Alpe di Siusi), Europe's largest high-altitude meadow, for scenic hiking.
- Take the cable car to panoramic viewpoints and enjoy a picnic surrounded by jagged peaks.

Day 3: Cortina d'Ampezzo and Lago di Braies

- Travel to Cortina d'Ampezzo, the "Queen of the Dolomites."
- Visit the iconic Lago di Braies, a pristine lake perfect for photography and leisurely walks.
- Spend the evening in Cortina, sampling local cuisine.

Day 4: Stelvio Pass and Bormio

- Drive along the Stelvio Pass, one of the most breathtaking mountain roads in the world.
- Relax in Bormio's thermal baths, known for their therapeutic properties.

Day 5: Adventure in Livigno

- Spend the day in Livigno, a hub for outdoor activities like mountain biking and zip-lining.
- Take advantage of duty-free shopping in the town center.

Day 6: Val di Funes and Charming Villages

- Explore the picturesque Val di Funes, famous for its idyllic scenery and St. Magdalena Church.
- Stop in nearby villages like Ortisei for art galleries and traditional crafts.

Day 7: Aosta Valley and Departure

- Visit Aosta, known for its Roman ruins and alpine charm.
- If time permits, tour a local vineyard or castle before heading home.

Weekend Getaways in the Alps

Short on time? A weekend in the Italian Alps can still offer unforgettable experiences.

Option 1: Romantic Escape in the Dolomites

- **Day 1:** Arrive in Cortina d'Ampezzo, explore the town, and enjoy a candlelit dinner.
- **Day 2:** Visit Lago di Misurina and hike the Tre Cime di Lavaredo trails for awe-inspiring views.

Option 2: Adventure and Relaxation in Bormio

- **Day 1:** Drive through the Stelvio Pass and spend the afternoon skiing or hiking.
- **Day 2:** Unwind in Bormio's natural thermal baths and explore the historic town center.

Option 3: Cultural Weekend in Trento and Val di Non

- **Day 1:** Discover Trento's Renaissance architecture and museums.
- **Day 2:** Explore Val di Non's apple orchards and visit Castel Thun for a glimpse into the region's history.

Customizing Your Journey

To tailor your trip to your interests, consider the following factors:

Seasonal Preferences:

- **Winter:** Focus on skiing destinations like Madonna di Campiglio or Livigno.
- **Summer:** Opt for hiking, cycling, or lake activities in areas like Seiser Alm or Val d'Ultimo.

Travel Pace:

- For a relaxed trip, choose fewer destinations and spend more time exploring each one.
- For an action-packed adventure, plan multiple short visits to different towns or parks.

Interests and Activities:

- **Nature Lovers:** Prioritize national parks such as Stelvio or Adamello Brenta.
- **History Buffs:** Include stops in Aosta and Trento to delve into Roman and medieval history.
- **Food Enthusiasts:** Focus on gastronomic hotspots like Bolzano and the Valtellina valley.

Group Dynamics:

- Families: Look for kid-friendly activities and accommodations, such as easy hiking trails or chalets with play areas.
- Couples: Seek out romantic hideaways like boutique chalets or lakeside resorts.
- Solo Travelers: Opt for hostels or guided tours to meet fellow adventurers.

Planning Tools and Resources

- Use apps like *Komoot* or *AllTrails* for mapping hiking and biking routes.
- Check local tourism websites for seasonal events and insider tips.
- Research public transport schedules if relying on trains or buses to get around.

Final Tips for Itinerary Planning

- **Factor in Travel Time:** Mountain roads and public transport can be time-consuming, so account for this when planning your daily activities.
- **Stay Flexible:** Weather conditions may impact outdoor plans, so have a backup activity in mind.
- **Book Early:** Accommodations and tours in the Italian Alps often fill up quickly during peak seasons.

With careful planning, your itinerary can encompass the best of the Italian Alps, whether you're seeking adventure, relaxation, or cultural immersion. By balancing structured plans with room for spontaneity, you'll create memories that last a lifetime.

Chapter 14. Hidden Gems of the Italian Alps

The Italian Alps, with their towering peaks, pristine lakes, and charming villages, offer an abundance of well-known destinations like Cortina d'Ampezzo, Madonna di Campiglio, and the Dolomites. However, beyond the popular spots lies a treasure trove of hidden gems—lesser-known destinations and unique experiences that allow travelers to explore the Italian Alps away from the crowds. These places offer an authentic, more intimate connection with the region's natural beauty, history, and culture. In this chapter, we'll uncover these hidden gems and suggest unique experiences that you won't find in typical travel guides.

Lesser-Known Destinations

While famous towns and ski resorts are well-established on travelers' itineraries, there are countless lesser-known destinations in the Italian Alps that are just as breathtaking and offer a more peaceful retreat.

1. Val di Funes (South Tyrol)
Nestled in the Dolomites, Val di Funes is a spectacular valley that often gets overshadowed by its more famous neighbors like Cortina d'Ampezzo. Known for its postcard-worthy landscapes, this charming valley is home to the iconic Church of St. Magdalena, with its backdrop of jagged peaks. It's a paradise for photographers, hikers, and those looking to escape the hustle and bustle. Hiking trails range from easy walks through lush meadows to more challenging treks up to breathtaking viewpoints. In winter, the area offers snowshoeing and cross-country skiing, with fewer crowds than more popular destinations.

2. Valle del Chiese (Trentino)
This quiet valley in the heart of Trentino is an excellent choice for travelers looking to immerse themselves in nature without the crowds. Valle del Chiese is known for its picturesque villages, clear mountain lakes, and scenic hiking trails. The area is perfect for exploring on foot or by bike. The **Lago di Idro**, located at the foot of the Alps, is a hidden gem for swimming, kayaking, or simply relaxing along the shores. The historic town of **Storo**, with its medieval architecture and peaceful atmosphere, offers a glimpse of local life in this under-the-radar corner of the Alps.

3. Aosta Valley (Val d'Aosta)
While the Aosta Valley is home to some more famous Alpine towns, it also offers plenty of hidden treasures. For instance, the **Gran Paradiso National Park**, located in the valley, is one of Italy's oldest protected areas and

provides hiking, wildlife spotting, and stunning views of the surrounding peaks. The quaint village of **Cogne**, nestled in the heart of the park, offers a serene escape with its beautiful Alpine architecture, and the town of **Aosta** itself has a mix of Roman ruins and medieval architecture waiting to be explored. The **Fenestrelle Fort**, a massive and impressive fortress, is another hidden gem that's not as widely visited but incredibly worth the trip.

4. Sappada (Friuli Venezia Giulia)
Located in the northeastern region of Italy, Sappada is a charming village that blends traditional Alpine architecture with a unique Austrian flair. This small town is famous for its wooden houses adorned with intricate carvings, making it a picturesque destination year-round. Visitors can enjoy outdoor activities like hiking in the summer and skiing or snowboarding in winter. The village is also home to an ancient carnival tradition, which involves elaborate masks and costumes. For those looking for an off-the-beaten-path experience, Sappada offers a peaceful and beautiful alternative to more tourist-heavy mountain resorts.

5. Cogne and the Gran Paradiso National Park (Aosta Valley)
Cogne, located in the Aosta Valley, offers a combination of Alpine charm and access to the **Gran Paradiso National Park**. While the park itself is well-known to locals and those in the know, it is still relatively undiscovered by international visitors. The area is a haven for wildlife enthusiasts, with ibex, chamois, and golden eagles often spotted during hikes. The town itself is a charming mix of stone houses, small cafes, and artisan shops. Winter in Cogne brings opportunities for

cross-country skiing and snowshoeing, while summer offers an array of hiking trails with panoramic views of snow-capped peaks.

Unique Experiences Off the Beaten Path

While the Italian Alps are known for skiing, hiking, and mountain sports, there are several unique experiences that are rarely found in the more crowded tourist destinations. These activities allow you to immerse yourself in the local culture and natural beauty in a way that's both intimate and unforgettable.

1. Cheese and Wine Tasting in Valtellina
Valtellina, a beautiful valley in Lombardy, is a haven for food lovers, and its lesser-known status makes it even more appealing for those seeking a more authentic experience. The region is famous for its cheeses, particularly **Bitto**, an ancient Alpine cheese made with a mix of cow's and goat's milk, and **Casera**, another local specialty. Combine this with a tasting of the region's wines—**Sforzato di Valtellina** is a particularly unique red wine produced from partially dried grapes—and you have a culinary experience that's sure to please. Many local farms and vineyards offer private tours and tastings, providing an opportunity to learn about traditional Alpine food production.

2. The Via Ferrata in Val di Mello
For those looking for an adrenaline-pumping adventure in the Italian Alps, a **via ferrata** (iron path) is an excellent way to combine hiking with rock climbing. One of the most thrilling, yet lesser-known, via ferrata routes

is found in **Val di Mello**, a stunning valley in the Lombardy region. Known for its pristine wilderness and dramatic granite cliffs, the valley offers a via ferrata that traverses steep walls, waterfalls, and alpine meadows. The experience is suitable for both beginners and experienced climbers, making it a fantastic way to connect with the Alps in a unique and thrilling way.

3. Ice Climbing in the Dolomites
While the Dolomites are a popular destination for skiing, they also offer fantastic opportunities for **ice climbing** in the winter months. This challenging and exhilarating activity is perfect for adventurers seeking something unique. The **Val di Fassa** and **Val di Fiemme** are home to several ice climbing routes, with frozen waterfalls and steep rock faces providing the ideal conditions. Beginners can take lessons from local guides, while experienced climbers can tackle more difficult routes. Ice climbing in the Dolomites offers a completely different perspective of the mountains, with stunning ice formations and breathtaking winter landscapes.

4. Snowshoeing in the Aosta Valley
Snowshoeing offers a slower-paced, but equally rewarding, way to explore the Italian Alps in winter. In the **Aosta Valley**, away from the crowded ski resorts, there are countless trails that wind through ancient forests, across frozen lakes, and up to high mountain viewpoints. Snowshoeing allows you to immerse yourself in the peace and quiet of the Alpine landscape, surrounded by snow-covered peaks. Popular snowshoeing areas include the **Gran Paradiso National Park** and **Valpelline**, where experienced guides can lead you on a tour of the area's untouched nature.

5. The Carnival of Ivrea

For a cultural experience that is completely off the beaten path, consider attending the **Carnival of Ivrea**, a centuries-old festival held in the small town of Ivrea in the Piemonte region. While not technically in the Alps, the event is closely associated with the Alpine culture of Northern Italy. The highlight of the carnival is the infamous **Battle of the Oranges**, where teams of locals throw oranges at one another in a high-energy and somewhat chaotic celebration. This unique event, along with traditional parades and performances, gives visitors a glimpse into the region's rich history and lively culture.

The hidden gems of the Italian Alps offer an unforgettable experience for those willing to step off the well-trodden path. From quiet valleys and charming villages to unique activities like ice climbing and cheese tasting, these lesser-known destinations and experiences reveal the heart and soul of the Alps. By venturing beyond the famous resorts and popular trails, you'll encounter a more intimate, authentic side of this stunning region, and create memories that will last a lifetime. Whether you're exploring a quiet valley, tasting local delicacies, or enjoying an adrenaline-packed adventure, the Italian Alps have something extraordinary to offer everyone.

Chapter 15. Sustainable Travel in the Alps

The Italian Alps are one of the most breathtaking natural landscapes in the world, attracting millions of visitors each year. As the demand for mountain adventures and alpine experiences continues to grow, it is more important than ever to adopt sustainable travel practices. The delicate balance between preserving the region's natural beauty, supporting local communities, and allowing tourists to explore these magnificent peaks and valleys requires thoughtful consideration. In this chapter, we'll explore eco-friendly practices, ways to support local communities, and how travelers can contribute to preserving the stunning natural landscapes of the Italian Alps.

Eco-Friendly Practices

Sustainable travel focuses on minimizing the negative environmental impact of tourism while maximizing the benefits to local economies and communities. As travelers, we have a responsibility to reduce our carbon footprint and be mindful of our surroundings. The Italian Alps, with their pristine forests, alpine meadows, and protected areas, are particularly vulnerable to the effects of mass tourism. Here are some eco-friendly practices to follow when exploring the Alps:

1. Using Public Transportation and Eco-Friendly Transport Options
The Italian Alps have a well-developed public transportation system, with buses and trains that connect most of the major towns and villages. Opting for public transport instead of driving a private car reduces carbon emissions and traffic congestion in these picturesque regions. The train journeys through the Alps offer a scenic and relaxing way to travel, allowing you to enjoy the landscape without the environmental cost of a car.

For those who prefer a more active approach, renting an electric bike (e-bike) is a great way to explore the Alps sustainably. Many towns, particularly in the South Tyrol and Trentino regions, offer e-bike rentals that allow you to cover more ground with less effort while reducing your environmental impact. Some regions also have an extensive network of dedicated cycling paths, making it easier and safer to explore without a car.

2. Minimizing Waste and Plastic Use
Reducing waste, particularly single-use plastics, is

another important aspect of sustainable travel in the Alps. Many Alpine destinations, especially in the more remote areas, are not equipped to handle large quantities of waste. Travelers can do their part by bringing reusable water bottles, packing reusable bags for shopping, and avoiding products that come with excessive packaging. When hiking, always pack out what you pack in to ensure that these natural environments stay pristine.

In addition, some ski resorts and Alpine towns are making strides in reducing plastic waste. Many are introducing initiatives such as refill stations for water bottles, encouraging visitors to purchase reusable items, and implementing waste sorting programs. As a responsible traveler, it's important to participate in these efforts and support businesses that prioritize sustainable practices.

3. Respecting Local Wildlife
The Alps are home to diverse ecosystems, from lush forests to alpine meadows, and a rich variety of wildlife. Respecting local wildlife is a key part of eco-friendly travel. While hiking or exploring the mountains, it's essential to keep a safe distance from animals and refrain from feeding them. Wild animals, including ibex, marmots, and golden eagles, thrive in these habitats because they are untouched by human interference. Disrupting their natural behavior by getting too close or feeding them can cause harm to the animals and the ecosystem.

Additionally, many Alpine areas have designated nature reserves or protected parks, such as **Gran Paradiso National Park** and **Stelvio National Park**, where wildlife is particularly vulnerable. Be sure to follow all park rules and respect the boundaries set for conservation. Avoid straying off marked trails to preserve the natural flora and fauna that thrive in these delicate environments.

Supporting Local Communities

Sustainable travel isn't just about environmental conservation; it's also about supporting the local communities that rely on tourism for their livelihoods. By choosing to engage with local businesses, travelers can contribute to the preservation of traditional customs, crafts, and ways of life. Here are some ways to support the people who call the Alps home:

1. Staying in Family-Owned Hotels and Inns
While large hotels and chains are common in Alpine resorts, opting to stay in locally owned accommodations—such as family-run inns, bed-and-breakfasts, or boutique hotels—ensures that your money directly benefits the local economy. These small, independent hotels offer a more personalized experience, where you can connect with local hosts who share their knowledge of the region's culture, history, and traditions. Additionally, many of these accommodations prioritize sustainability, using local materials, energy-efficient systems, and eco-friendly practices.

2. Dining in Local Restaurants
The food of the Italian Alps is one of the region's greatest treasures. From hearty mountain fare to delicate alpine cheeses, local cuisine reflects the flavors of the land. When dining in the Alps, choose family-

owned trattorias, restaurants, and mountain huts that source ingredients locally. These eateries often feature dishes made with produce from nearby farms, providing a direct benefit to the surrounding agricultural community. Eating locally also supports farmers and artisans who produce traditional products like cheese, wine, and cured meats.

Don't forget to try regional specialties such as **speck** (smoked ham), **canederli** (bread dumplings), and **fondue** (melted cheese). Supporting restaurants that prioritize seasonal, locally grown food helps preserve traditional farming practices and reduces the carbon footprint associated with food transport.

3. Participating in Local Crafts and Markets
In many towns and villages in the Italian Alps, local markets are a hub for handcrafted goods and artisanal products. From woolen scarves and hand-carved wooden figurines to alpine herbs and locally produced cheeses, these markets offer a range of products that reflect the region's culture and traditions. Purchasing locally made goods ensures that artisans and farmers are fairly compensated for their work. Moreover, buying unique handcrafted items is an excellent way to take home a piece of the Alps while contributing to the preservation of traditional craftsmanship.

In some areas, you can also participate in workshops or guided tours to learn about local crafts and trades. For instance, you might find a workshop where you can learn how to make your own wooden ski poles or take a cooking class to learn how to prepare traditional Alpine dishes.

Preserving the Natural Beauty

One of the greatest reasons to visit the Italian Alps is their pristine natural beauty—towering peaks, sparkling lakes, lush valleys, and ancient forests. Preserving this beauty is a collective responsibility shared by locals, businesses, and visitors. Here are some ways travelers can actively help preserve the natural environment:

1. Responsible Hiking and Skiing Practices
The Italian Alps are a paradise for outdoor enthusiasts, with hiking, skiing, and other activities attracting visitors year-round. However, outdoor recreation can have a significant environmental impact if not practiced responsibly. When hiking, always stick to designated trails and avoid shortcuts, as trampling off-path can damage sensitive ecosystems. In addition, be mindful of weather conditions, as hiking during snowmelt or in heavy rain can cause erosion of the trails and harm the surrounding environment.

For skiers, consider choosing resorts that prioritize sustainable skiing practices, such as using energy-efficient lifts, reducing snowmaking, and managing waste. Some resorts in the Alps are working to improve their environmental credentials by adopting sustainable practices like using renewable energy and promoting green construction.

2. Participating in Conservation Initiatives
Several environmental organizations and Alpine parks offer opportunities for visitors to contribute to conservation efforts. You can participate in guided eco-tours, volunteer for wildlife monitoring projects, or take part in tree planting initiatives aimed at restoring forest

areas affected by deforestation or fire. These activities not only benefit the environment but also provide a deeper understanding of the region's conservation efforts.

3. Sustainable Ski Resorts
In recent years, several ski resorts in the Italian Alps have adopted sustainable practices. Resorts such as **Val di Fiemme** and **Alta Badia** have made efforts to reduce their environmental footprint by using energy-efficient technologies, building eco-friendly accommodations, and implementing waste-reduction initiatives. Skiers can contribute to preserving the environment by selecting these sustainable resorts, as they focus on minimizing their impact while still offering world-class skiing experiences.

Sustainable travel in the Italian Alps is about making mindful choices that respect both the environment and local communities. By adopting eco-friendly practices, supporting local businesses, and contributing to the preservation of natural beauty, travelers can ensure that this incredible region remains unspoiled for future generations. The Italian Alps offer a wealth of natural wonders, cultural experiences, and outdoor adventures, and by traveling sustainably, you can help protect these treasures while creating lasting memories. Whether you're hiking, skiing, or simply enjoying the landscape, every action you take can contribute to the ongoing preservation of the Italian Alps, one of the world's most awe-inspiring destinations.

Chapter 16. Practical Information and Resources

When planning a trip to the Italian Alps, having the right practical information can make all the difference in ensuring a smooth and enjoyable journey. Whether you're navigating language barriers, managing your budget, or knowing where to seek help in case of an emergency, understanding these key aspects of your travel experience will help you make the most of your time in this stunning region. In this chapter, we'll provide essential resources for navigating the Italian Alps, covering language, currency, budgeting, and emergency contacts.

Language and Communication

The official language of the Italian Alps, like the rest of Italy, is Italian. However, given the region's proximity to several European countries and its international appeal, you'll find that many locals speak some level of English, especially in popular tourist areas, ski resorts, and mountain towns. That said, it's always a good idea to learn a few basic Italian phrases to enhance your travel experience and show respect for the local culture.

1. Common Italian Phrases for Travelers
Knowing a few key phrases in Italian can go a long way in making interactions smoother, especially when visiting more remote villages where English is less commonly spoken. Here are some useful phrases to help you get by:

- **Ciao** (Hello/Goodbye)
- **Buongiorno** (Good morning)
- **Buonasera** (Good evening)
- **Per favore** (Please)
- **Grazie** (Thank you)
- **Dove si trova…?** (Where is…?)
- **Quanto costa?** (How much does it cost?)
- **Mi scusi, parli inglese?** (Excuse me, do you speak English?)
- **Aiuto!** (Help!)

Learning these basic phrases can make it easier to ask for directions, order food, or engage with locals. In addition to Italian, you may hear German or Ladin in certain areas of the Alps, particularly in regions like South Tyrol (Bolzano, Merano), where German is an official language alongside Italian. Ladin is spoken by a small minority in some mountain valleys.

2. Mobile Phones and Internet Access
Mobile phone coverage in the Italian Alps is generally good, especially in the larger towns and ski resorts. However, as you venture into more remote areas or higher altitudes, the signal may become weaker or intermittent. It's recommended to check with your mobile service provider about international roaming charges before you leave.

For those staying in major Alpine resorts or cities, Wi-Fi is commonly available in hotels, restaurants, and cafes. Most Alpine destinations have sufficient internet access, but it's always wise to check with your accommodation in advance if you require reliable access. Some more isolated villages may have limited internet connectivity, so plan accordingly if you need consistent access for work or communication.

3. Translation Apps
If you're not fluent in Italian, download a translation app to help bridge the gap. Apps like Google Translate or Duolingo can help with basic communication and offer translation features that work offline, which is especially useful in remote areas where Wi-Fi may be limited. These apps allow you to translate signs, menus, or conversations in real-time, making it easier to navigate the region and communicate with locals.

Currency, Costs, and Budgeting

The currency used in the Italian Alps is the **Euro (€)**, which is the official currency of Italy. Whether you're staying in a chic ski resort, a cozy alpine village, or an urban center, prices across the Alps can vary significantly depending on the region, the time of year, and the type of activity you're engaging in. Here's an overview of the costs you can expect while traveling in the Italian Alps.

1. General Cost of Living
Generally, the Italian Alps can be more expensive than other parts of Italy, particularly in tourist-heavy areas like Cortina d'Ampezzo, Bolzano, and some ski resorts. However, it is still possible to travel to the Alps on a variety of budgets. Major cities and popular ski resorts will have a higher cost of accommodation, dining, and activities. A luxury hotel room in a top-tier ski resort can easily cost upwards of €200–€300 per night, while a mid-range hotel might be priced between €80–€150 per night. On the other hand, more budget-friendly accommodations such as hostels, guesthouses, or alpine B&Bs may offer rates starting at €50–€70 per night.

Dining out in the Italian Alps can be quite affordable, especially in smaller villages. A meal at a casual trattoria can cost between €15 and €30 per person, while dining at a fine-dining restaurant may cost upwards of €50 per person or more, especially if you are indulging in regional specialties like truffles, fondue, or wine pairings.

2. Skiing and Outdoor Activities
The cost of skiing in the Italian Alps can vary greatly based on the resort, the time of year, and the length of your stay. A single ski pass typically ranges from €40 to €60 per day, depending on the resort and the number of lifts available. Ski rental costs (for skis, poles, and

boots) can also add up, with prices typically ranging from €25 to €40 per day.

For other outdoor activities, like hiking, cycling, or sightseeing, costs can vary. Many Alpine trails and natural parks have free access, but some attractions (such as cable car rides, guided tours, or entry fees to national parks) may have small fees. Guided day trips can range from €50 to €100, depending on the activity.

3. Tipping and Gratuities
Tipping in Italy is not mandatory, but it is appreciated for good service. In restaurants, rounding up the bill or leaving a 5–10% tip is common, although most restaurants include a service charge (called **coperto**) in the final bill, especially in larger cities or tourist areas. In cafes and bars, it's customary to leave a small tip of €1–€2 if you've had table service.

For taxi drivers or private drivers, rounding up the fare or leaving a small tip is also appreciated. For tour guides, a tip of €5–€10 per person is generally acceptable, depending on the length of the tour and the quality of service.

Emergency Contacts and Travel Services

While the Italian Alps are known for their natural beauty and outdoor activities, it's important to be prepared in case of an emergency. Whether you're hiking, skiing, or simply enjoying the landscapes, knowing who to contact and where to go for help can give you peace of mind during your travels.

1. Emergency Numbers
The emergency numbers for Italy are:

- **112**: European emergency services number (ambulance, fire, police)
- **118**: Medical emergency services for ambulances
- **115**: Fire department
- **113**: Police
- **118**: Mountain rescue services (for ski accidents or mountain-related emergencies)

Emergency services in the Italian Alps are highly responsive, especially in popular tourist areas. In remote areas, be prepared for a longer response time, as mountainous terrain can make access difficult. Most ski resorts and alpine hotels will have their own emergency protocols in place and will be able to assist in the event of an accident or medical issue.

2. Medical Care
In case of illness or injury, you can visit a **farmacia** (pharmacy), which is readily available in most towns and villages. For more serious medical issues, it's important to go to a local hospital or health center. Major towns such as Bolzano, Trento, and Aosta have well-equipped hospitals with English-speaking staff, and ski resorts often have medical clinics for on-site treatment.

For tourists, it's a good idea to have travel insurance that covers medical care and emergency evacuation, particularly if you plan on skiing or hiking in remote areas. Travel insurance can help cover the cost of medical treatment, as well as any associated costs like evacuation or repatriation in case of serious injury.

3. Tourist Information Centers
Tourist information centers are located in most major towns, resorts, and national parks. These centers are invaluable resources for travelers, providing maps, brochures, and recommendations for activities, dining, and accommodations. In addition to information about things to do, staff at these centers can also offer advice on transportation, weather conditions, and safety guidelines for outdoor activities.

In popular regions such as South Tyrol, Trentino, and the Dolomites, many tourist centers offer multilingual services, making it easier for visitors from around the world to get the information they need.

Having access to the right practical information is key to making the most of your time in the Italian Alps. By learning a few basic phrases in Italian, understanding the cost of living and budgeting for your trip, and knowing where to turn in case of an emergency, you can ensure that your Alpine adventure is both enjoyable and stress-free. Whether you're soaking in the region's natural beauty, savoring its local cuisine, or taking part in outdoor activities, this guide to practical resources will help you make the most of your time in one of Italy's most stunning regions.

Chapter 17.Final Thoughts: Embracing the Magic of the Italian Alps

The Italian Alps are a place where nature's beauty and the allure of Italian culture merge seamlessly. Whether you're drawn to the snow-capped peaks, the charming alpine villages, the rich culinary traditions, or the thrill of outdoor adventures, this region offers something for every traveler. The Italian Alps are not just a destination; they are an experience—one that invites you to immerse yourself in breathtaking landscapes, rich history, and a way of life that values both relaxation and adventure in equal measure. In this final chapter, we reflect on the essence of the Italian Alps, why it should be at the top of your travel list, and how it will continue to inspire and captivate future visitors.

Reflections on the Region

The Italian Alps are more than just a geographical feature; they are a symbol of timeless beauty, resilience, and cultural diversity. Stretching across northern Italy, the Alps form an awe-inspiring natural boundary, offering an abundance of experiences that cater to all types of travelers. From the towering peaks of the Dolomites, which are recognized as a UNESCO World Heritage Site, to the tranquil valleys of South Tyrol, where Italian and German cultures converge, the region is an extraordinary blend of nature, history, and modern life.

What makes the Italian Alps truly special is the way it allows visitors to experience contrasting worlds within a single region. During the winter months, world-class ski resorts like Cortina d'Ampezzo and Sestriere transform into bustling hubs of activity, offering unparalleled skiing and snowboarding experiences. When the snow melts, the mountains reveal their summer splendor—lush meadows, wildflower-filled valleys, and winding trails perfect for hiking, mountain biking, and scenic drives. It's a destination that changes with the seasons, offering new reasons to return year after year.

In addition to its natural wonders, the Italian Alps are home to a rich tapestry of traditions and cultures. From the Ladin-speaking valleys to the German-speaking communities of South Tyrol, there is an incredible diversity of customs, dialects, and cuisines. This cultural fusion adds depth to the region, making it not only a beautiful place to explore but also a place of deep historical significance.

The charm of the Italian Alps also lies in its smaller, lesser-known destinations. While places like Bolzano, Merano, and Aosta are well-known, it is in the quieter, tucked-away towns and villages where you may discover the true heart of the region. These spots offer authenticity, simplicity, and a slower pace of life that is often lost in more tourist-heavy locations. These hidden gems, such as the villages in the Val di Fassa or the small towns in the Susa Valley, allow travelers to experience the Alps in its most unspoiled form.

Why the Italian Alps are a Must-Visit

The Italian Alps should be on every traveler's bucket list, and for good reason. They provide a perfect combination of outdoor adventure, relaxation, culture, and cuisine—all set in one of the most visually stunning locations in the world.

First and foremost, the Alps are an adventure-lover's paradise. Skiing, snowboarding, mountaineering, and hiking are just a few of the outdoor activities that draw millions of visitors each year. Whether you're an experienced skier tackling the slopes of the Dolomites or a casual hiker exploring the scenic trails of the Stelvio National Park, the Alps offer activities for every level of adventurer. The mountain resorts are well-equipped with state-of-the-art infrastructure, making it easy to indulge in these pursuits while enjoying the comfort and convenience of modern amenities.

Secondly, the Italian Alps are a destination that allows for an immersive cultural experience. From the fine wines and alpine cheeses to the traditional Tyrolean music and festivals, there is an authenticity here that you won't find in more touristy destinations. The local people take immense pride in their heritage, and they are always eager to share it with visitors. Whether it's sampling the rich flavors of local cuisine or attending a traditional Alpine festival, the cultural experiences are as rich as the natural beauty that surrounds you.

Thirdly, the Alps are a destination that caters to all types of travelers. For those seeking luxury, the region boasts five-star resorts, private chalets, and gourmet restaurants offering panoramic mountain views. For those on a more budget-conscious trip, there are plenty of affordable accommodations, from charming guesthouses to cozy mountain huts, ensuring that everyone can enjoy the magic of the Italian Alps. Whether you're traveling solo, as a couple, or with family, there are experiences here that are both relaxing and exhilarating.

Lastly, the Italian Alps are a must-visit for anyone looking to experience Italy in its purest form. While cities like Rome, Florence, and Venice offer a wealth of cultural treasures, the Alps provide a more tranquil yet equally fascinating side of the country. The region gives travelers the opportunity to connect with nature, discover picturesque towns, and enjoy the slower pace of life that is so often associated with rural Italy. It's the perfect antidote to the hustle and bustle of more crowded destinations.

Encouragement for Future Adventures

As you plan your visit to the Italian Alps, keep in mind that this is a destination meant to be savored slowly. There is no rush to cover everything in one trip. The beauty of the Alps lies in its ability to surprise you at every turn. The winding mountain roads, the serene lakes tucked away in valleys, and the welcoming villages all beckon you to pause and take it all in.

Whether it's your first visit or your tenth, the Italian Alps will continue to offer new adventures and discoveries. You may find yourself returning for the skiing in the winter, the hiking in the summer, or the autumn harvest festivals in small villages. Each season brings its own unique charm, making it a destination that can be enjoyed year-round. The Alps are also a place that invites reflection. Standing at the foot of a snow-capped peak, listening to the wind rustling through the pines, or watching a golden sunset over the valleys, you'll experience moments of serenity that will stay with you long after your trip has ended.

For those planning their first visit, take your time to explore the diverse regions that make up the Italian Alps. Whether you're skiing in the Dolomites, hiking in Trentino, or enjoying a peaceful village in Aosta Valley, the region offers a richness that can't be fully experienced in a single trip. And don't be afraid to step off the beaten path—while the major towns and resorts are undoubtedly spectacular, it's the lesser-known destinations that often leave the greatest impression.

To those who have already experienced the magic of the Italian Alps, know that there are always more treasures to discover. From hidden valleys and unspoiled lakes to quiet mountain villages and new trails, the Alps have an endless supply of beauty waiting to be explored.

The Italian Alps are a place of adventure, relaxation, and cultural discovery. Their allure lies not only in their natural beauty but also in the experiences they offer— from skiing and hiking to food, wine, and heritage. It's a destination that can be enjoyed by anyone, no matter their interests or travel style. With each visit, you'll find new reasons to fall in love with this magical region. So, pack your bags, embrace the adventure, and let the Italian Alps enchant you. Whether you're seeking thrilling outdoor activities or a peaceful escape in nature, the Italian Alps promise to deliver an unforgettable experience. The mountains are calling—are you ready to answer?